主 编◎吴勇毅　　副主编◎刘　弘

School: _____

Grade/Class: _____

Name: _____

# China Study 5

# 中国研习

刘艳辉　王佳艺◎译

Nicholas Thomas Zazzi ◎审

华东师范大学出版社

# 编写说明

　　《中国研习》是一套为国际学校1–12年级外籍学生开发的中国文化与社会探究教材。本套教材的编写参考了IB课程大纲，并且吸收了教育部基础教育课程教材发展中心（NCCT）"外籍人员子女学校认证标准"中有关中国文化课程教学的要求。教材采取探究式教学方法，并为该课程研发了数字教育平台，力求创造轻松愉快的学习环境，培养学生开放的、包容的批判性思维能力。

　　全套教材共分成小学、初中和高中三个系列。小学系列共有6册，初中和高中系列各有3册。每册有12个单元，每个单元涉及一个主题，教师可以根据学校的课时安排每周或者若干周学习一个单元，也可以根据教学需要挑选其中某个单元来使用。

　　本套教材具有如下几个主要特点：

**1. 以主题方式编写教材**

　　主题式教学是以内容为载体、以文本的内涵为主题所进行的一种教学活动。本套教材的主题尽量考虑到国际学校学生在学习、生活中可能会遇到的各种社会文化内容，并且有意识养成学生能对母国文化和中国文化进行比较和思考的习惯，以培养学生的国际情怀。

**2. 以探究式活动来组织教材内容编排，便于师生使用**

　　中国研习作为一门跨学科探究性课程，兼顾学科内的知识和跨学科领域的知识。为此，本套教材在呈现方式上以探究、活动等多维度方式为主，而非传统的简单的内容灌输施教形式；强调在各种探究活动中帮助学生内化吸收相关的知识和能力，包括不同学科的知识；鼓励学生成为学习的主体，教师则在学生的学习中起到有效的引导作用。

**3. 教材所涉及的中国文化和社会的领域十分广泛**

　　为适应国际学校有关中国社会及文化课程的需要，本套教材所涉及的内容不仅仅局限于狭义的中国文化范畴，而是扩展到中国艺术（包括音乐、戏剧、视觉艺术等），政治，经济，历史，地理，科学（包括数学、物理、化学等）等多方面，这与IB课程要跨学科、内容要涉及多种学科领域的理念是一致的。我们认为，中国文化教学不仅是中文教师的工作，其他学科的教师也完全可以参与其中，也唯有如此，才能真正使得文化通识在国际教育环境下扎根。这种跨学科的教学，也符合IB等国际教育中强调的"课程融合"理念。

### 4. 提供具体的评价指标，便于教师对于学生的表现作出评价

为了适应活动探究的教学需要，本套教材鼓励教师以过程化的档案袋评价方式为主。教师通过对学生在不同阶段的学习过程和学习结果进行评估，及时对学生的学习表现作出反馈并提出改进意见，从而在教学过程中更好地激发学生的兴趣，调动学生的学习主动性，引导他们学习、理解、研究和探索，让学生成为主导自己的主人。

### 5. 中英文对照编辑，适应多种需要

考虑到国际学校学生汉语水平和课程教学的多样性特点，本套教材采取中英文对照形式，这样既可以满足国际学校基于内容的汉语教学的需要，也可以供国际学校教授其他课程的教师参考或补充教学，还可以作为师生的课外活动手册。此外，教材中将重要文化知识和内容要点列出，也便于学生自学使用。

本套教材的研发团队来自华东师范大学等知名高校和多所国际学校，不仅包括拥有丰富教学经验和较高理论水平的高校专业教师，还吸收了一部分国际学校一线的教学和管理人员。其核心成员参加过国际汉语教学相关标准、大纲和教材的研发工作，对于各类国际学校常用标准、大纲和课程有过专门研究，在国内外发表过相关的研究成果，具有丰富的课程设计和教材编写经验。

希望通过学习和使用本套教材，能够使更多的国际学生认识中国、了解中国。

吴勇毅

2018 年 8 月

# Editor's Words

China Studies is a set of Chinese culture and social inquiry textbooks designed for foreign students of international schools in grades 1–12. Based on the IB syllabus, this set of textbooks has absorbed the teaching requirements of "certification standards of school for foreign children" developed by National Center for School Curriculum and Textbook Development Ministry of Education (NCCT). The textbooks adopt an exploration-based teaching method and provide a digital education platform, attempting to create a relaxing and enjoyable learning environment and to develop students' critical thinking skills.

This set of textbooks is divided into three series: elementary school, junior high school and senior high school. There are 6 volumes in the elementary school series and 3 volumes in the junior high school and senior high school series respectively. There are 12 units in each volume and every unit deals with a specific theme. Teachers can teach one unit for each week or several weeks according to class schedule, or select one of the units to use according to requirements.

This set of textbooks has the following main features:

## 1. Theme-related teaching method

Theme-related teaching method is based on the content and the connotation of each unit. This set of textbooks takes into account the various social cultural contents that international school students may encounter in their study and life, and intends to cultivate students' habit of comparing and thinking about their native culture and

Chinese culture in order to cultivate their international feelings.

### 2. Exploratory activities to facilitate teachers' and students' use

China Studies is an interdisciplinary exploration course that intends to incorporate knowledge within the discipline and knowledge in interdisciplinary fields. To this end, this set of textbooks is based on exploration, activities and other multi-dimensional ways rather than simply cramming knowledge into students' heads. We emphasize on students' ability to absorb knowledge of different subjects through various exploration activities. We also encourage students to become the initiator of learning and teachers to play an effective guiding role in students' learning.

### 3. Covering a wide range of Chinese culture and society

In order to meet the needs of the international school curriculum on Chinese society and culture, the content of this set of textbooks is not limited to the narrow Chinese culture category but extended to Chinese art (including music, opera, visual arts, etc.), politics, economy, history, geography, science (including mathematics, physics, chemistry, etc.) and many other aspects—consistent with the concept that IB courses should be interdisciplinary and involve multiple subjects. We believe that Chinese culture teaching is not only the work for Chinese teachers, and teachers from other disciplines can also participate in Chinese culture teaching. Only in this way can cultural education take root in an international education environment. This interdisciplinary teaching is also in line with the "curricular integration" concept emphasized in international education such as IB.

**4. Providing specific evaluation means for students' performance**

In order to meet the needs of activity exploration, this set of textbooks encourages teachers to focus on process evaluation. Teachers evaluate students' learning process and results at different stages, and give timely feedback and suggestions to students' learning performance so as to evoke students' interest in study and guide them to further understand, research and explore Chinese culture.

**5. Editing in both Chinese and English to meet various needs**

Taking into consideration the diversity of Chinese language proficiency and curriculum teaching in international schools, this set of textbooks offers both English and corresponding Chinese translations. This can meet the needs of content-based Chinese language teaching in international schools, as well as the needs of international school teachers who teach other courses. It can also be used as a manual for extracurricular activities. In addition, important cultural knowledge and content points are listed in the textbook, which is also convenient for students to study by themselves.

The writers of this set of textbooks come from well-known universities such as ECNU and many international schools. They include professional teachers with rich teaching experience and high theoretical level, and also some front-line teaching and management personnel from international schools. Among them, the core members have participated in the development of relevant standards, syllabus and textbooks for international Chinese teaching and have conducted special research on these fields with relevant results published at home and abroad.

We hope that by studying and using this set of materials, more international students can get to know China and understand China better.

August 2018

# 目录

**第一课**
**Lesson One**
交通工具 / 12
Transportation Means / 13

**第二课**
**Lesson Two**
《三字经》/ 20
*Three Character Classic* / 21

**第三课**
**Lesson Three**
中国货币 / 28
Chinese Currency / 29

**第四课**
**Lesson Four**
广播体操和广场舞 / 40
Broadcast Exercises and Square Dance / 41

**第五课**
**Lesson Five**
中国古代计时方法 / 46
Methods of Time-Keeping in Ancient China / 47

**第六课**
**Lesson Six**
端午节 / 56
The Dragon Boat Festival / 57

# Contents

**第七课**
**Lesson Seven**

中国民乐 / 66
Chinese Folk Music / 67

**第八课**
**Lesson Eight**

中国画 / 74
Chinese Painting / 75

**第九课**
**Lesson Nine**

中国航天事业 / 84
Chinese Aerospace Projects / 85

**第十课**
**Lesson Ten**

拔河 / 92
Tug of War / 93

**第十一课**
**Lesson Eleven**

泥塑和面人 / 98
Clay Sculptures and Dough Figurines / 99

**第十二课**
**Lesson Twelve**

茶 / 106
Tea / 107

## 1. 学习目标

（1）知道中国主要的交通工具类型。

（2）了解各种交通工具的特点。

## 2. 热身活动

### 想一想

（1）什么是交通工具?

（2）你知道哪些交通工具的名称?

### 说一说

你坐什么交通工具来上学?

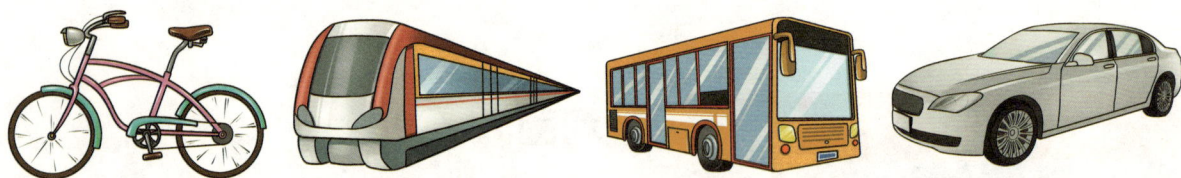

## 3. 阅读课文

### 交通工具的作用

　　交通工具是人类生活中不可缺少的一部分。随着时代的变化和科技的进步，我们周围的交通工具越来越多，给人们的生活带来了极大的便利。交通工具大大缩小了人们的交往

# Lesson One  Transportation Means

## 1.  Learning objectives

(1) Know the main methods of transportation in China.

(2) Observe the characteristics of different transportation means.

## 2.  Warm-up

### Thinking

(1) What is transportation means?

(2) What transportation means do you know?

### Speaking

Which kind of transportation do you take to school?

## 3.  Reading texts

### Functions of Transportation Means

Transportation is an indispensible part of human life. With changing times and progress in science and technology, more and more vehicles are around us, which

距离，节约了人们的出行时间，"日行千里"早已不再是无法实现的梦想。

## 各种各样的交通工具

现代中国的交通工具多种多样，主要有自行车、公共汽车、地铁、私家车、高铁和飞机。

自行车环保方便，但是速度比较慢，所以现在很多人骑自行车不是为了出行，而是为了锻炼身体。

公共汽车是在城市道路上按照固定路线运行的机动车辆。公共汽车通常只有一层，也有双层公共汽车。公共汽车能到达很多地方，车费便宜，是人们出行最常用的交通工具。

地铁原来指在地下运行的城市轨道交通系统，现在也包括在地面上运行的轻轨。地铁不会堵车，装载量大，非常方便快捷。在中国的一些城市中还有磁悬浮列车，与地铁相比，它的速度更快。

很多家庭现在都拥有了私家车，人们出行不受时间限制，非常方便。但是近几年来，私家车数量剧增，这加重了道路拥挤和空气污染。

如果要去比较远的地方，可以选择长途汽车、高铁或者飞机。长途汽车最便宜，但是速度较慢。高铁方便快捷，安全性高，价格也不太贵。飞机的价格比较昂贵，但是它的速度是交通工具中最快的。

brings great convenience. It is the automobile that brings people together and helps us save travel time. Covering a thousand miles in a day is no longer an unattainable dream.

## Various Transportation Means

There are various methods of transportation in modern China, including bicycles, buses, subways, private cars, high-speed trains, and airplanes.

It's convenient and environmentally-friendly to travel by bicycle. Owing to the low speed, many people choose to ride bicycles for exercise rather than travel.

Buses are motor vehicles that travel according to fixed routes in the streets of cities. Usually there is only one deck for a bus, but there are also double-decker buses. Bus is the most popular vehicle because it can reach almost everywhere and the fare is usually quite cheap.

Subways originally refer to the underground railways, and now also include light-rail trains that travel above the ground. With large capacity, subways are very convenient and swift and free of traffic jams. In some Chinese cities there are also maglev trains that are even faster.

Many families own private cars and travel is no longer limited by time. But in recent years, the increasing number of cars makes both road congestion and air pollution even worse.

When travel to remote places, you can take the long-distance bus, high-speed train, or airplane. The long-distance bus is the cheapest with low speed. The high-speed train, being convenient and swift with excellent security, is not very expensive. However, the airplane, which is really expensive to take, is the fastest among all the vehicles.

## 4. 重点词汇

交通工具　地铁　火车　高铁　自行车　公共汽车

## 5. 实践活动

**想一想**

（1）假设你和爸爸妈妈想在周末从上海出发去南京玩。坐高铁大约需要1.5小时，每张票的价格大约为140元；坐汽车大约需要4小时，每张票的价格大约为105元；坐飞机大约需要1小时，每张票的价格大约为400元。你会选择哪种交通工具？为什么？

（2）交通工具给我们的生活带来了许多便利，同时也带来了一些烦恼，比如噪音、堵车、空气污染等。你有什么解决上述问题的办法吗？

（3）未来的交通工具还会有什么变化？说说你的想法。

**画一画**

画出你最喜欢的交通工具，并为它写一段"自我介绍"。

## 4. Keywords

transportation means   subway   train   high-speed train   bicycle   bus

## 5. Activities

### Thinking

(1) Suppose you plan to go to Nanjing for the weekend with your parents. It takes you about 1.5 hours from Shanghai to Nanjing by high-speed train, about 140 yuan for each ticket. It takes you about 4 hours by long-distance bus, 105 yuan per person. By airplane, it takes about 1 hour, at 400 yuan per ticket. Which transportation method will you choose and why?

(2) Vehicles have brought us both convenience and trouble, such as noise, traffic jams, and air pollution. Do you have any solutions to the problems?

(3) What will happen to the vehicles in the future? Share your opinion with the rest of the class.

### Drawing

Draw a picture of your favorite transportation vehicle and write a self-introduction for it.

## 6. 自我评估

| | 😊 | 😐 | 😞 |
|---|---|---|---|
| （1）我知道中国有各种各样的交通工具。 | | | |
| （2）我能说出不同交通工具的特点。 | | | |
| （3）我能根据情况选择合适的交通工具。 | | | |

## 6. Self-assessment

| | 😊 | 😐 | 😣 |
|---|---|---|---|
| (1) I know various kinds of transportation means in China. | | | |
| (2) I can tell the characteristics of different types of transportation means. | | | |
| (3) I can choose the right means of transportation according to the situation. | | | |

# 第二课 《三字经》

## 1. 学习目标

（1）了解《三字经》的道德意义。

（2）能讲述课文中的《三字经》小故事。

## 2. 热身活动

### 说一说

（1）你小时候读过哪些书？你最喜欢哪一本？为什么？

（2）看一段《三字经》的朗读视频。这段视频的内容有什么特点？主要讲述什么？

## 3. 阅读课文

### 《三字经》简介

　　《三字经》是中国的传统启蒙教材，来源于古代中国的文学、历史、哲学、天文地理、人伦义理、忠孝节义等，所以中国人有"熟读《三字经》，可知千古事"的说法。《三字经》和《百家姓》、《千字文》并称为"三大国学启蒙读物"。

# Lesson Two    *Three Character Classic*

## 1.  Learning objectives

(1) Know the morals of *Three Character Classic*.

(2) Be able to tell the stories from *Three Character Classic*.

## 2.  Warm-up

### Speaking

(1) What books did you read when you were a kid? Which one was your favorite and why?

(2) Watch a video clip about the recital of *Three Character Classic*. What are the features of the video clip? What's the main idea?

## 3.  Reading texts

### Introduction to *Three Character Classic*

*Three Character Classic* is a traditional enlightenment textbook in China. Its resources are from ancient Chinese literature, history, philosophy, geography, ethics, loyalty, filial piety, and justice. Therefore, there is a saying in China, "Read *Three Character Classic* well and you can know the old things." *Three Character Classic*, *Hundred Family Surname*s, and *Thousand Character Classic* are called the three most important national enlightenment readings.

## 昔孟母，择邻处

孟子小的时候和母亲住在墓地旁边。孟子常常和邻居的小孩一起学大人跪拜、大声哭叫的样子，玩办理丧事的游戏。孟子的母亲看到了，觉得这里不适合孟子居住，就带着孟子搬到了市集。到了市集，孟子又和邻居的小孩学商人做生意和屠宰猪羊的样子。孟子的母亲知道了，又觉得这里不适合孟子居住，于是他们搬到了学校附近。每月初一，官员到孔子庙行礼跪拜，以礼相待，孟子见了之后学习并且记住了这些礼节。孟子的母亲很高兴，觉得这才是孟子应该居住的地方，于是在这里住了下来。

## 香九龄，能温席

黄香小时候，家中生活很苦难，他9岁时母亲就去世了。冬天晚上黄香读书的时候，觉得特别冷。他想，这么冷的天气，父亲白天干了一天的活，晚上还不能好好地睡觉，实在太辛苦了。小黄香为了让父亲晚上睡觉时不冷，他读完书便悄悄走进父亲的房里，给他铺好被子，然后钻进父亲的被窝里，用自己的体温温暖了冰冷的被窝之后，才让父亲睡下。

## 4. 重点词汇

三字经　启蒙　孟母三迁

## Mencius' Mother Chose the Neighborhood

Mencius lived with his mother near a graveyard when he was a little child. He was often playing by building tombs or imitating others crying for the dead. Mother thought this was not good, so they moved to live near the market. However, Mencius also imitated other people doing business and killing pigs and goats. Mother thought that this was not good either, so they moved again next to a school. On the first day of each lunar month, the officials would come to the Confucius Temple in the school to perform the prostration ceremony toward the Confucius statue. Mencius learned etiquette and knowledge from this. Mother thought that was what the children should learn, and she felt very happy and no longer moved.

## When Huang Xiang Was Nine, He Could Warm
## the Mat for His Father

When Huang Xiang was a child, his life was difficult. His mother passed away when he was nine. In the winter, he felt extremely cold as he studied at night. Thinking that his father couldn't have a sound sleep under such chilliness after a day's hard work, he felt very sorry for his father. Therefore, he made a bed for his father and lied in his freezing quilt to make it warm by his own body. Only after doing this would he let his father sleep in the warm quilt.

## 4. Keywords

*Three Character Classic*   enlightenment   Mencius' mother moving her house three times

## 5. 实践活动

### 演一演

分角色，表演孟母三迁的故事。

### 说一说

（1）你的国家有类似孟母三迁的故事吗？

（2）你觉得孟子母亲的做法对吗？你认为环境对人的影响大吗？为什么？

### 画一画

把你最喜欢的《三字经》故事画成漫画。

### 做一做

给你的父母制作一张感恩卡。

## 5. Activities

### Acting

Role-play the story "Mencius' Mother Moving Her House Three Times".

### Speaking

(1) Is there such a story similar to "Mencius' Mother Moving Her House Three Times" in your country?

(2) Do you think Mencius' mother is correct or not? Do you agree that environment has strong impact on a person? Why?

### Drawing

Choose your favorite story from *Three Character Classic* and make it into a comic.

### Practicing

Make a gratitude card for your parents.

## 6. 自我评估

| | 😊 | 😐 | ☹️ |
|---|---|---|---|
| （1）我知道《三字经》是中国的传统启蒙教材。 | | | |
| （2）我能讲述一个《三字经》小故事。 | | | |
| （3）我能在生活中做到敬老爱幼。 | | | |

## 6. Self-assessment

| | 😊 | 😐 | ☹️ |
|---|---|---|---|
| (1) I know that *Three Character Classic* is a traditional Chinese enlightenment textbook. | | | |
| (2) I can tell one story from *Three Character Classic*. | | | |
| (3) I respect the aged and cherish the young. | | | |

## 1. 学习目标

（1）认识中国古代和近现代重要的钱币。

（2）了解中国钱币博物馆的情况。

## 2. 热身活动

**说一说**

（1）你见过哪些中国钱币？

（2）你去过哪些博物馆？你印象最深刻的是哪一个？为什么？

## 3. 阅读课文

### 人　民　币

人民币（缩写：RMB）是中华人民共和国的法定货币，由中国人民银行于1948年开始发行。到目前为止共发行过五套人民币，现在市场上使用的主要为第五套人民币。

### 中国古代钱币

中国古代钱币种类很多，多为金属铸币，上面还多有文字标记。从秦到清，主要使用方孔的铜质圆钱，但从宋到金、元、明、清，和铜钱一起使用的还有纸币和银锭。

# Lesson Three  Chinese Currency

## 1. Learning objectives

(1) Know the important Chinese currencies of both ancient and modern times.

(2) Learn about China Numismatic Museum.

## 2. Warm-up

### Speaking

(1) What kinds of Chinese numismatics have you seen?

(2) What museums have you been to? Which museum leaves the deepest impression on you? Why?

## 3. Reading texts

### Renminbi

Renminbi (abbreviated as RMB) is the official currency of the People's Republic of China, and was first issued by the People's Bank of China in 1948. Up to now five sets of RMB have been issued. At present, the fifth set of RMB is in circulation.

### Ancient Chinese Numismatics

There were various numismatics in ancient China, mostly metal, with Chinese characters on them. From the Qin dynasty to the Qing dynasty, a kind of round bronze coin with a square in the center was used. Paper currency and silver ingot were added to the bronze coins from the Song dynasty to the Jin, Yuan, Ming and Qing dynasties.

（1）秦半两。

（2）汉代马蹄金。

（3）唐朝"顺天元宝"大钱（背上仰月纹）。

（4）北宋"圣宋元宝"（行书长字）铜钱。

(1) Half-liang coin, Qin dynasty.

(2) Hoof-shaped gold, Han dynasty.

(3) "Shun Tian Yuan Bao" large bronze coin (with upward moon pattern on the back), Tang dynasty.

(4) "Sheng Song Yuan Bao" (of cursive script) bronze coin, Northern Song.

（5）北宋"交子"。北宋"交子"是中国最早由政府正式发行的纸币，也被认为是世界上最早使用的纸币。

（6）宋朝"京销锭银"二十五两银铤。

（7）明朝"洪武通宝"背"福"折十大钱。

(5) Jiao Zi, Northern Song. Jiao Zi is the earliest paper currency issued by the government in China, and is also considered as the earliest paper currency in the world.

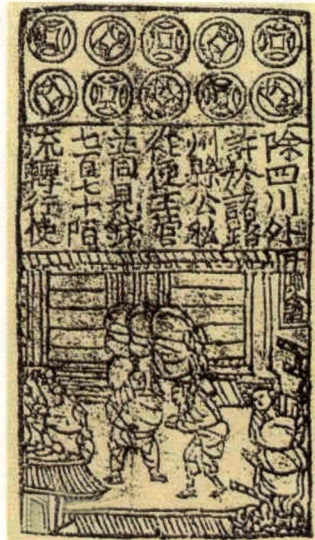

(6) "Jing Xiao Ding Yin" 25-liang silver ingot, Northern Song.

(7) "Hong Wu Tong Bao" 10-wen large bronze coin with the character *fu* on the back.

（8）大明通行宝钞（壹贯），"户部"。

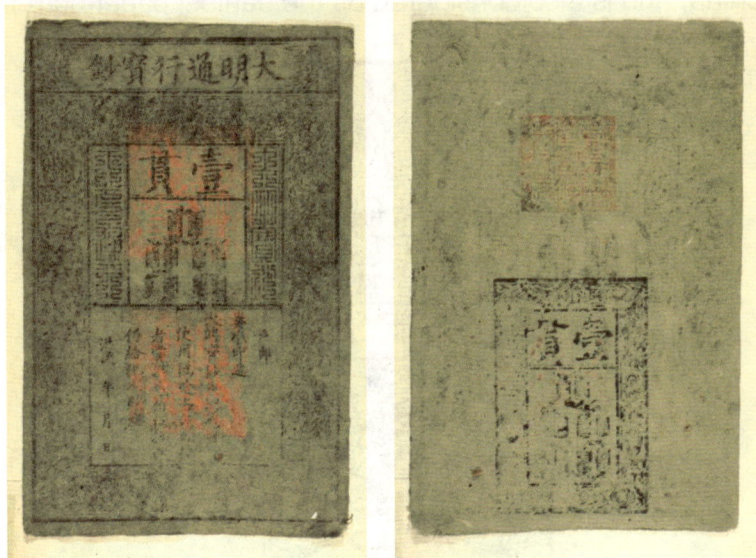

（9）清朝"道光重宝"宝源局母钱。

## 中国钱币博物馆

位于北京市的中国钱币博物馆成立于1992年，收藏了古代、近现代货币及银行史相关实物，藏品约30余万件，按古钱币、金银币、纸币、少数民族钱币、外国钱币、钱范及

(8) "Da Ming Tong Xing Bao Chao" paper money, 1-guan, Hu Poo, the Board of Revenue.

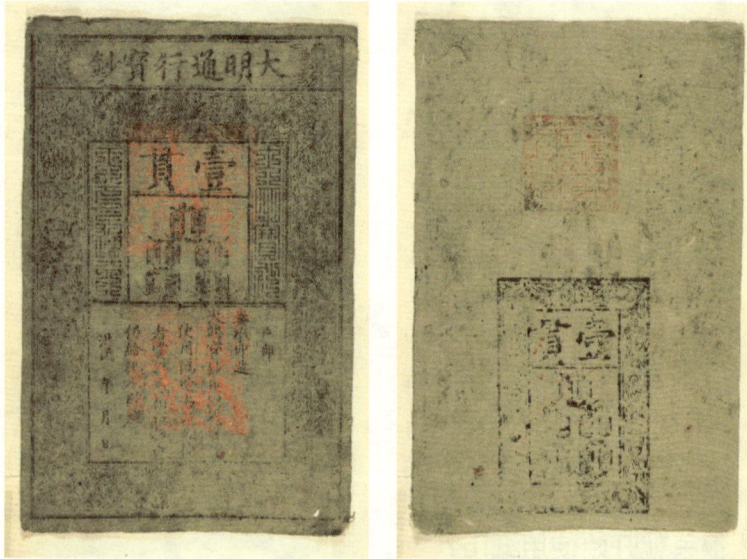

(9) "Dao Guang Zhong Bao" model brass coin of Baoyuan Burean, Qing dynasty.

## China Numismatic Museum

Located in Beijing, China Numismatic Museum was founded in 1992. It has a collection of numismatics from ancient and modern times and objects related to the history of banks. There are more than 300,000 collections in the museum, which are sorted and stored according to the classification of ancient coins, gold and silver coins, paper currencies, coins of minorities, foreign coins, coin molds, and antiques

与钱币有关的文物等六大类别整理、收藏和保管。中国钱币博物馆的陈列有"中国历代货币陈列"、"中国古代铸钱工艺展"和"中国人民银行行史展"等。

## 4. 重点词汇

钱币　人民币　交子

## 5. 实践活动

### 想一想

为什么中国人很早就开始使用纸币？

### 说一说

（1）中国古代的钱币在形状上有什么特点？

（2）不同材质的钱币有什么优点和缺点？

（3）中国古代钱币与你的国家的古代钱币有哪些异同？

### 做一做

（1）开办一个"跳蚤"市场，销售和购买旧物。

（2）收集中国钱币的资料，制作一个展板，向大家介绍不同的钱币。

related to coins. The museum's exhibitions include "Chinese Currencies from Successive Dynasties", "Ancient Chinese Coin-casting Technology", and "History of The People's Bank of China".

## 4. Keywords

numismatic    RMB    Jiao Zi

## 5. Activities

### Thinking

Why could the Chinese use paper money so early in time?

### Speaking

(1) What shapes are the ancient Chinese numismatics?

(2) What are the advantages and disadvantages of numismatics made of different materials?

(3) What are the similarities and differences between the ancient numismatics of China and those of your own country?

### Practicing

(1) Open a flea market, buying and selling second-hand goods.

(2) Collect materials about ancient Chinese numismatics, and make a panel to introduce them.

## 6. 自我评估

|  | 😊 | 😐 | ☹️ |
|---|---|---|---|
| （1）我能说出中国古代钱币的特点。 |  |  |  |
| （2）我能说出中国古代钱币和西方古代钱币的异同。 |  |  |  |
| （3）我能说出最早使用纸币的国家名字。 |  |  |  |

## 6. Self-assessment

| | 😊 | 😐 | 😞 |
|---|---|---|---|
| (1) I can tell the characteristics of ancient Chinese numismatics. | | | |
| (2) I can tell the similarities and differences between ancient Chinese numismatics and Western ones. | | | |
| (3) I know which country is the first to use paper currencies in the world. | | | |

# 第四课　广播体操和广场舞

## 1. 学习目标

（1）知道中国人喜欢集体活动。

（2）了解广播体操和集体舞。

（3）了解中国大妈经常做的集体活动——跳广场舞。

（4）学一段广播体操或者集体舞。

## 2. 热身活动

**看一看**

观看北京奥运会和伦敦奥运会的开幕式片段。它们的表演风格有何不同？

## 3. 阅读课文

### 中国人喜欢集体活动

受地理环境、历史环境和政治环境的影响，中国一直是一个盛行集体主义的国家。在古代，人们奉行以"忠"、"孝"为核心的伦理观念，把父子君臣、兄弟朋友、夫妻五伦紧紧联系在一起，实行大一统。在社会主义的新中国，人们也相信团结力量大、众人拾柴火焰高。所以，中国人喜欢集体活动。

# Lesson Four   Broadcast Exercises and Square Dance

## 1.  Learning objectives

(1) Understand that Chinese people enjoy collective activities.

(2) Learn about broadcast exercises and group dance.

(3) Know the collective activity enjoyed by older Chinese ladies, the square dance.

(4) Learn to perform broadcast exercises or group dance.

## 2.  Warm-up

### Watching

Watch the opening ceremony of the Beijing Olympic Games with that of the London Olympic Games in the video clips. What are the differences in performance style?

## 3.  Reading texts

### Chinese People Love Collective Activities

Owing to its unique geographic, historic, and political circumstances, China is a country that cherishes collectivism. In ancient times, people pursued the ethical concepts of loyalty and filial piety, connecting father-son, monarch-subject, husband-wife relationships and even relations between brothers and friends with feudal order, thus grand unification was achieved. In modern China, people believe in unity, embracing the idea that great things may be done by mass effort. Therefore, Chinese people enjoy collective activities.

### 广播体操

广播体操是一种很有中国特色的全民体育运动。广播体操不需要专门的运动设备，对场地也没有太多要求，只要跟随广播或者口令就可以进行锻炼，是中国人非常重要的健身方式。广播体操是中小学生们的课间操，也是企事业单位工作人员的工间操，曾经百万人同做广播体操的景象令人难忘。

### 集 体 舞

集体舞是一种大众性的舞蹈，舞步相对简单，队形变换也不复杂，容易开展，有助于丰富人们的业余文化生活。近年来，国家大力推行中小学生集体交谊舞。相较于广播体操而言，集体舞更富有舞蹈的美感，对身体协调性要求更高，也对男女学生正常交往有着有益的影响。

### 广 场 舞

广场舞是近几年中国非常流行的一种群众性的健身活动。广场舞的主要参与人群是中老年人，其中又以大妈为主。广场舞的音乐通常都是时下的流行歌曲，舞步都比较简单。随着参与广场舞的人越来越多，一首曲子还会有很多个不同的舞蹈版本。

## Broadcast Exercises

Broadcast exercises are unique all-the-people sports with Chinese characteristics which require neither special sport facilities nor large space. What you do need is to follow the directions from the broadcast and do the corresponding exercises. Broadcast exercises are the major way of fitness for Chinese people and now become the physical exercises during breaks for both primary school students and employees. The scene of a million people do broadcast exercises together is really great and unforgettable.

## Group Dance

Group dance is a kind of popular dance. Its dance steps are simple without many formation changes, thus it's easy to perform and can enrich people's leisure life. Recently, group social dances have been practiced vigorously among primary and middle school students. Compared with broadcast exercises, group dance is more graceful and requires a better physical coordination of the performers. It is also a positive way of communication between boys and girls.

## Square Dance

Square dance is a popular mass body building activity in China in recent years. The major participants of the square dance are middle-aged and old people, especially women. The music for square dance is usually pop songs and the movement is usually simple. With more and more people participating in the square dance, one song can have multiple dance versions.

## 4. 重点词汇

广播体操　集体舞　广场舞

## 5. 实践活动

**想一想**

为什么中国人喜欢集体活动？

**说一说**

（1）在你的国家，人们喜欢集体活动吗？

（2）在你的国家，学生做广播体操吗？

（3）你觉得现在的年轻人喜欢广播体操或者集体舞吗？为什么？

（4）广播体操和集体舞你更喜欢哪一个，为什么？

**做一做**

跟着视频或者跟着老师学做几节广播体操。

## 6. 自我评估

| | 😊 | 😐 | ☹️ |
|---|---|---|---|
| （1）我知道中国人喜欢集体活动。 | | | |
| （2）我能说出广播体操的名称。 | | | |
| （3）我会做几节广播体操。 | | | |
| （4）我知道集体舞和广场舞的特点。 | | | |

## 4. Keywords

broadcast exercises   group dance   square dance

## 5. Activities

### Thinking

Why do Chinese people enjoy collective activities?

### Speaking

(1) Do people in your country like collective activities?

(2) Do the students in your country do broadcast exercises?

(3) Do you think young people today like broadcast exercises or group dance? Why or why not?

(4) Which one do you prefer, broadcast exercises or group dance?

### Practicing

Learn to perform some segments of broadcast exercises following video clips or your teacher.

## 6. Self-assessment

| | ☺ | 😐 | ☹ |
|---|---|---|---|
| (1) I understand that Chinese people enjoy collective activities. | | | |
| (2) I can tell the names of broadcast exercises. | | | |
| (3) I can do several segments of broadcast exercises. | | | |
| (4) I can tell the characteristics of group dance and square dance. | | | |

# 第五课　中国古代计时方法

## 1. 学习目标

（1）了解中国古代的计时方法。

（2）了解中国古代的计时工具。

（3）了解中外计时方法和计时工具的不同。

## 2. 热身活动

### 说一说

现在是几点？你是怎么知道现在的时间的？

### 想一想

如果古代人想要知道时间，他们该怎么做？你知道自己国家古代的计时工具吗？

## 3. 阅读课文

### 中国古代计时单位

中国古代把一天24小时分为12个时辰，每个时辰2小时，23:00-1:00为子时，后面依次为丑时、寅时、卯时、辰时、巳时、午时、未时、申时、酉时、戌时、亥时。中国古

# Lesson Five　Methods of Time-Keeping in Ancient China

## 1. Learning objectives

(1) Know the time-keeping methods of ancient China.

(2) Know the tools of time-keeping in ancient China.

(3) Know the similarities and differences in time-keeping methods and tools between China and other countries.

## 2. Warm-up

### Speaking

What time is it now? How do you know?

### Thinking

What would ancient people do if they wanted to know the exact time? Do you know anything about the time-keeping tools of your country in ancient times?

## 3. Reading texts

### Time-Keeping Units in Ancient China

In ancient China, the 24 hours of a day was divided into 12 periods, each of which lasted for 2 hours. For example, 23:00 p.m.–1:00 a.m. is called *zǐ shí*, then followed by *chǒu shí*, *yín shí*, *mǎo shí*, *chén shí*, *sì shí*, *wǔ shí*, *wèi shí*, *shēn shí*, *yǒu*

代还有把一夜分为五更的做法，每更为一个时辰，戌时为一更、亥时为二更、子时为三更、丑时为四更、寅时为五更，由此可以知道，中国人常说的"半夜三更"就是指23:00-1:00这段时间。此外，因为计时工具不同，古代中国人还用过"刻"等计时单位。

| 子时 | 23:00-01:00 | 子初 | 23:00 | 夜半 | 又名"子夜"、"中夜"，十二时辰的第一个时辰 |
| | | 子正 | 00:00 | | |
| 丑时 | 01:00-03:00 | 丑初 | 01:00 | 鸡鸣 | 又名"荒鸡"，十二时辰的第二个时辰 |
| | | 丑正 | 02:00 | | |
| 寅时 | 03:00-05:00 | 寅初 | 03:00 | 平旦 | 又名"黎明"、"早晨"、"日旦"等，是夜与日的交替之际 |
| | | 寅正 | 04:00 | | |
| 卯时 | 05:00-07:00 | 卯初 | 05:00 | 日出 | 又名"日始"、"破晓"、"旭日"等，指太阳刚刚露脸、冉冉初升的那段时间 |
| | | 卯正 | 06:00 | | |
| 辰时 | 07:00-09:00 | 辰初 | 07:00 | 食时 | 又名"早食"等，古人"朝食"之时也就是吃早饭的时间 |
| | | 辰正 | 08:00 | | |
| 巳时 | 09:00-11:00 | 巳初 | 09:00 | 隅中 | 又名"日禺"等，临近中午的时候 |
| | | 巳正 | 10:00 | | |
| 午时 | 11:00-13:00 | 午初 | 11:00 | 日中 | 又名"日正"、"中午"等 |
| | | 午正 | 12:00 | | |
| 未时 | 13:00-15:00 | 未初 | 13:00 | 日昳 | 又名"日跌"、"日央"等，太阳偏西为日跌 |
| | | 未正 | 14:00 | | |
| 申时 | 15:00-17:00 | 申初 | 15:00 | 晡时 | 又名"日晡"、"夕食"等 |
| | | 申正 | 16:00 | | |

*shí*, *xū shí*, and *hài shí*. There was also another method in ancient China to divide the night into five stages, each of which is called a *gēng*. Each stage is equivalent to two hours. For example, *xū shí* is the same as *yī gēng*, *hài shí* as *èr gēng*, *zǐ shí* as *sān gēng*, *chǒu shí* as *sì gēng* and *yín shí* as *wǔ gēng*. Therefore, the Chinese phrase "*sān gēng* of the mid-night" refers to the period of 23:00 p.m.–1:00 a.m. In addition, the ancient Chinese also used *kè* and other time-keeping units due to the existence of different time-keeping tools.

| | | | | | |
|---|---|---|---|---|---|
| *zǐ shí* | 23:00–01:00 | *zǐ chū* | 23:00 | Mid-night | The first period of the twelve |
| | | *zǐ zhèng* | 00:00 | | |
| *chǒu shí* | 01:00–03:00 | *chǒu chū* | 01:00 | Crow | The second period of the twelve |
| | | *chǒu zhèng* | 02:00 | | |
| *yín shí* | 03:00–05:00 | *yín chū* | 03:00 | Daybreak | The alternate of night and day |
| | | *yín zhèng* | 04:00 | | |
| *mǎo shí* | 05:00–07:00 | *mǎo chū* | 05:00 | Sunrise | The time when the sun just rises |
| | | *mǎo zhèng* | 06:00 | | |
| *chén shí* | 07:00–09:00 | *chén chū* | 07:00 | Food time | Also called "morning eating" which refers to breakfast time |
| | | *chén zhèng* | 08:00 | | |
| *sì shí* | 09:00–11:00 | *sì chū* | 09:00 | Close to noon | The period close to noon |
| | | *sì zhèng* | 10:00 | | |
| *wǔ shí* | 11:00–13:00 | *wǔ chū* | 11:00 | Noon | Also called "mid-noon" |
| | | *wǔ zhèng* | 12:00 | | |
| *wèi shí* | 13:00–15:00 | *wèi chū* | 13:00 | Sundown | The period that the sun has gone west |
| | | *wèi zhèng* | 14:00 | | |
| *shēn shí* | 15:00–17:00 | *shēn chū* | 15:00 | Afternoon | Also called "afternoon-snack time" |
| | | *shēn zhèng* | 16:00 | | |

（续表）

| 酉时 | 17:00-19:00 | 酉初 | 17:00 | 日入 | 又名"日落"、"日沉"、"傍晚"，意为太阳落山的时候 |
|---|---|---|---|---|---|
| | | 酉正 | 18:00 | | |
| 戌时 | 19:00-21:00 | 戌初 | 19:00 | 黄昏 | 又名"日夕"、"日暮"、"日晚"等，此时太阳已经落山，天将黑未黑，天地昏黄，万物朦胧 |
| | | 戌正 | 20:00 | | |
| 亥时 | 21:00-23:00 | 亥初 | 21:00 | 人定 | 又名"定昏"等，此时夜色已深，人们也已经停止活动，安歇入睡了 |
| | | 亥正 | 22:00 | | |

## 漏　　刻

　　漏刻是中国古代运用最广的一种计时工具，漏是指高处的滴水壶，刻是指低处的收水壶中央的刻度尺（相当于现代钟表的表盘）。在下方的收水壶中有一个浮标，浮标上有一支箭，箭尾指示的刻度尺上的刻度就是此时的时刻。漏刻把一天分为96刻，一刻相当于15分钟。

## 日　　晷

　　日晷，即太阳的影子，是利用太阳的投影方向来计量时间的一种工具，在中国已有三千多年的历史。日晷由平行于赤道的晷面和垂直于晷面的晷针组成。晷面相当于现代钟表的表盘，晷针在晷面上落下的影

(Continued)

| yǒu shí | 17:00–19:00 | yǒu chū | 17:00 | Sunset | Also called "nightfall" which refers to the period when the sun goes down |
|---------|-------------|---------|-------|--------|----------------------------------------------------------------------------|
|         |             | yǒu zhèng | 18:00 |        |                                                                          |
| xū shí | 19:00–21:00 | xū chū | 19:00 | Evening | The period that the sun has already set and the sky darkened |
|        |             | xū zhèng | 20:00 |         |                                                              |
| hài shí | 21:00–23:00 | hài chū | 21:00 | Night | The period that the night is deep and the people are sleeping |
|         |             | hài zhèng | 22:00 |       |                                                               |

## The Clepsydra

The clepsydra was the most widely used time-keeping tool in ancient China. *Lòu* refers to the water bottle placed on a higher place while *kè* refers to the scale at the center of the lower bottle collecting water from the one above (equivalent to the dial of a modern clock). There is an arrow on the buoy at the collection bottom, and the number on the scale indicated by the arrow stands for the present time. The clepsydra divides one day into 96 *kè*; every unit is equal to 15 minutes.

## The Sundial

The sundial, which literally means the shadow of the sun, is a tool to measure time by using the projected direction of the sun, and was first used in China more than three thousand years ago. The sundial is made up of the sundial surface, parallel to the equator, and the sundial needle, perpendicular to the sundial surface. The surface is equivalent

子指示了当时的时刻。随着西式钟表的引进，日晷由于体积较大、质量重且不能在阴雨天气使用逐渐失去了作为时间计量工具的功能，但作为时间的象征，它依旧伫立在各式宫殿门前。

## 4. 重点词汇

时辰　更　刻　日晷

## 5. 实践活动

### 想一想

（1）在你的国家，古代有哪些计时方法？你还知道哪些国家古代的计时方法？它们的计时单位分别是什么？

（2）如果在野外没有手表和其他现代设备，你该怎么判断时间？

### 做一做

制作一个日晷模型，看看它是否可以用来判断时间。

### 说一说

（1）漏刻和日晷这样的计时工具有什么优缺点？

to the dial of the modern timepiece, and the shadow of the sundial needle on the sundial surface indicates the time. With the introduction of Western clocks, the sundial has gradually lost its function as a time measuring tool, because of its larger size, heavy weight, and inability to be used in rainy days. But as a symbol of time, it still stands in front of the gates of various palaces.

## 4. Keywords

time period  *gēng*  *kè*  sundial

## 5. Activities

### Thinking

(1) What were the time-keeping methods from the ancient times of your country? What time-keeping methods do you know in other countries? What are the time-keeping units they use?

(2) How can you tell the time without a watch or other modern facilities in the wilderness?

### Practicing

Make a sundial model and see if it can be used to show time.

### Speaking

(1) What are the advantages and disadvantages of the time-keeping tools such as clepsydra and sundial?

（2）日晷和现代钟表有什么相同点和不同点？

**画一画，写一写**

设计一款计时工具，并写出它的功能介绍。

## 6. 自我评估

|  | ☺ | 😐 | ☹ |
|---|---|---|---|
| （1）我知道中国古代的计时方法。 | | | |
| （2）我知道时辰、更、刻的意义。 | | | |
| （3）我能说出几个中国古代时间计量工具的名称。 | | | |
| （4）我知道中外计时方法和计时工具的不同。 | | | |

(2) What are the similarities and differences between sundials and modern clocks?

## Drawing and Writing

Design your own time-keeping tool and write down its instructions.

## 6. Self-assessment

| | ☺ | 😐 | ☹ |
|---|---|---|---|
| (1) I know the time-keeping methods used in ancient China. | | | |
| (2) I know the meanings of time period, *gēng*, and *kè*. | | | |
| (3) I can say the names of the time-keeping tools in ancient China. | | | |
| (4) I can tell the differences in time-keeping methods and time-keeping tools between China and other countries. | | | |

# 第六课　端午节

## 1. 学习目标

（1）了解端午节及其来源。

（2）了解端午节的食物、活动。

（3）学会包粽子。

## 2. 热身活动

**说一说**

（1）你知道端午节吗？端午节中国人要做什么活动？

（2）端午节与哪个中国古人有关？今年的端午节在哪一天？

（3）你的国家有这样的节日吗？有哪些节日习俗？

## 3. 阅读课文

### 端午节的来源

每年的农历五月初五是中国的端午节。端午节，又称"五月节"、"端阳节"，是中国的传统节日之一，也是世界非物质文化遗产。关于端午节的起源，民间有很多种说法，纪

# Lesson Six　The Dragon Boat Festival

## 1.　Learning objectives

(1) Learn about the Dragon Boat Festival and its origin.

(2) Learn about the food and activities of the Dragon Boat Festival.

(3) Learn to make rice dumplings.

## 2.　Warm-up

### Speaking

(1) Do you know about the Dragon Boat Festival? What kinds of activities do Chinese people do during the Dragon Boat Festival?

(2) Who is the ancient Chinese person relevant to the Dragon Boat Festival? What is the date for Dragon Boat Festival this year?

(3) Do you have a similar festival in your country? What customs are concerned with it?

## 3.　Reading texts

### The Orgin of the Dragon Boat Festival

The fifth day of the fifth lunar month is the Chinese Dragon Boat Festival, also known as May Festival or Duanyang Festival. It is one of the traditional Chinese festivals and a world cultural heritage. There are various folk sayings about the origin of the Dragon Boat Festival. The most popular one is to commemorate Qu Yuan,

念伟大的爱国主义诗人屈原是最流行的一种。端午节有很多民俗活动，其中包粽子、赛龙舟最为有名。

## 粽　　子

粽子是端午节的代表食品，用粽叶包裹糯米蒸制而成，馅料丰富多样，不同地方的粽子差别很大。中国北方多食甜粽，馅料用白糯米加上蜜枣、蜜豆等，蘸糖食用，以北京粽子为代表。中国南方多食咸粽，馅料用拌了酱油的糯米加上蛋黄、鲜肉等，以嘉兴粽子为代表。相传，古时候人们会把捆好的粽子丢入江中，这样鱼儿就会来吃粽子而不会吃屈原的身体，以此来达到纪念屈原的目的。

## 赛　龙　舟

赛龙舟是端午节最重要的民俗活动之一。相传赛龙舟也是为了纪念屈原，赛龙舟发出的声音可以驱赶鱼类，让它们不再吃屈原的尸体。其实，早在战国时代，中国就有"龙舟

who was a great patriotic poet from over 2,000 years ago. This festival also involves many activities, the most famous ones include making rice dumplings and holding dragon boat races.

## Rice Dumplings

The rice dumpling is the special food for the Dragon Boat Festival. It is steamed with glutinous rice wrapped with reed leaves. Fillings are rich and vary greatly from place to place. Sweet rice dumplings are popular in northern China. The stuffings are made with white glutinous rice, candied dates, honey beans, and so on. They are eaten with sugar and represented by Beijing rice dumplings. In southern China, people eat salty rice dumplings, stuffed with glutinous rice mixed with soy sauce, egg yolk, pork, and so on, with Jiaxing rice dumplings as the representative. According to legend, in ancient times, in order to commemorate the great poet Qu Yuan, people would throw rice dumplings into the river, so that the fish would come to eat them instead of Qu Yuan's body.

## Dragon Boat Racing

The Dragon boat racing is one of the most important folk activities of the Dragon Boat Festival. According to legend, dragon boat racing is also held to commemorate Qu Yuan. The sound of dragon boat racing can drive away fish, so that they will not eat Qu Yuan's body. In fact, as early as the Warring States period, China had the

竞渡"的传统。水手坐在刻有龙头、龙尾的狭长独木舟上，跟着鼓手急促的鼓点声快速向前滑行。现在的龙舟比赛除了纪念屈原之外，还有更多的竞技性色彩，每年端午节前后中国都会举办大型的国际龙舟邀请赛。

## 端午节的其他风俗

中国农历五月份时，天气渐渐变热，蚊虫增多，食物容易变坏，因此端午节有许多习俗都与卫生习惯有关。比如沐兰汤，即全家老少都用艾叶、蒲叶等熬煮出药水洗浴，可以消暑辟邪。又如饮雄黄酒或在室内喷洒雄黄酒，或用雄黄酒末在小孩儿额头画"王"字，可以杀菌驱虫。此外还有系五色丝线、佩香囊、采艾草等习俗。

## 4. 重点词汇

农历　端午节　龙舟　粽子

## 5. 实践活动

### 想一想

人们为什么要包粽子？

tradition of holding dragon boat races. The sailors were seated in long, narrow dragon-shaped canoes, and followed the drummer's rapid drumming. The dragon boat racing now has more competitive spirits than commemorating Qu Yuan. Every year around the Dragon Boat Festival, the Chinese will hold a large international dragon boat race.

### Other Customs Concerned with the Dragon Boat Festival

The weather in the fifth month of the Chinese traditional calendar warms up gradually with an increasing number of flies and mosquitoes, as food turns bad easily. Thus many customs of the Dragon Boat Festival are related to health habits. For example, taking a bath with water made from steaming moxa and cattail leaves in order to relieve summer heat and keep away evil spirits. Other customs include drinking realgar wine, spraying it indoors, or drawing the Chinese character "王" which means "king" on a child's forehead with it, in order to kill the vermin and bacteria. In addition, there are also customs such as tying five-color silk threads, wearing perfume pouches and collecting moxa leaves.

## 4. Keywords

lunar calendar   the Dragon Boat Festival   dragon boat   rice dumpling

## 5. Activities

### Thinking

Why do people make rice dumplings?

# 中国研习

**说一说**

（1）包粽子需要哪些材料？

（2）你喜欢哪一种馅料的粽子？为什么？

（3）你划过船吗？你觉得划船难在哪里？

（4）你看过赛龙舟吗？你觉得最有意思的地方在哪里？

**认一认**

下列图片代表了哪些风俗？

**做一做**

（1）跟老师学习包粽子，把包好的粽子带回家和家人一起分享品尝。

（2）制作五彩丝线或者香囊。

**看一看**

观看《舌尖上的中国》第二季《主食的故事》粽子部分。

## Speaking

(1) What kinds of materials are used for making rice dumplings?

(2) What kind of rice dumplings do you like the best? Why?

(3) Have you ever rowed a boat? What is the most difficult part?

(4) Have you ever watched a dragon boat race? What is the most interesting part?

## Observing

What kinds of customs do the following pictures represent?

## Practicing

(1) Learn to make rice dumplings with your teacher and bring those you have made back home to share with your family.

(2) Make five-color silk threads or perfume pouchs.

## Watching

Watch the program *Rice Dumplings, The Staple Food* from the second season of the TV series *A Bite of China*.

## 6. 自我评估

| | 😊 | 😐 | 😞 |
|---|---|---|---|
| （1）我了解端午节及其来源。 | | | |
| （2）我知道端午节的民俗活动。 | | | |
| （3）我知道端午节要吃的食物的名字。 | | | |
| （4）我会包粽子。 | | | |

## 6. Self-assessment

| | 🙂 | 😐 | ☹️ |
|---|---|---|---|
| (1) I know about the Dragon Boat Festival and its origin. | | | |
| (2) I can tell the folk customs concerned with the Dragon Boat Festival. | | | |
| (3) I can tell the name of the food eaten during the Dragon Boat Festival. | | | |
| (4) I can make rice dumplings. | | | |

# 第七课　中国民乐

## 1. 学习目标

（1）了解中国民乐的主要特点。

（2）了解中国的民间乐器。

（3）学会欣赏经典的中国民乐。

## 2. 热身活动

### 说一说

（1）你常听什么类型的音乐？

（2）在你的国家，民乐指什么？

（3）你的国家的人喜欢民乐吗？在哪个场合能听到民乐？

（4）你家里人喜欢听民乐吗？

（5）你听过中国民乐吗？对中国民乐了解吗？

## 3. 阅读课文

### 中国民间乐器

中国民间乐器种类多样，可分为如下几种。

# Lesson Seven  Chinese Folk Music

## 1.  Learning objectives

(1) Know the main features of Chinese folk music.

(2) Know some Chinese folk instruments.

(3) Learn to appreciate classical Chinese folk music.

## 2.  Warm-up

### Speaking

(1) What kind of music do you often listen to?

(2) What is "folk music" in your country?

(3) Do people in your country enjoy folk music? Where can you hear this kind of music?

(4) Do your family members like folk music?

(5) Have you ever listened to any Chinese folk music? Do you know anything about it?

## 3.  Reading texts

### Chinese Folk Instruments

There are various folk instruments in China and they are divided into the following categories.

打击乐器：鼓。

吹管乐器：笛。

弹拨乐器：古筝、琵琶。

拉弦乐器：二胡。

## 中国民间乐器的历史

　　中国民间乐器有很长的历史。西周到春秋战国时期，民间流行吹笙、吹竽、鼓瑟、击筑、弹琴等器乐演奏形式，如秦汉的鼓吹乐，魏晋的清商乐，隋唐的琵琶音乐，宋代的细乐、清乐，元明的十番锣鼓、弦索等，演奏形式丰富多样。近代中国民间乐器的各种体裁和形式，都是传统形式的继承和发展。

Percussion instrument: drum.

Wind instrument: flute.

Plucked instruments: zither, pipa.

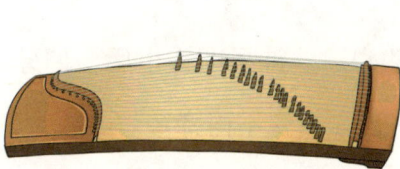

Stringed instrument: erhu.

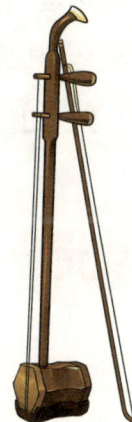

### History of Chinese Folk Instruments

Chinese folk instruments have a long history. From the Western Zhou dynasty to the Spring and Autumn and the Warring States period, lutes and pipe instruments were popular among average folks. In addition, the wind and percussion music of the Qin and Han dynasties, the Qingshang music of the Wei and Jin dynasties, the pipa music of the Sui and Tang dynasties, the silk and bamboo music of the Song dynasty, as well as the Shifan drum in Yuan and Ming dynasties are all traditional performance styles, and the origins of modern music genres and performances.

## 经典的中国民乐曲目
### ——《高山流水》的故事

伯牙善长弹琴，钟子期善于倾听。伯牙弹琴的时候，心里想到高山，钟子期说："好啊！简直就像高大的泰山屹立在我的面前！"心里想到流水，钟子期又说："好啊，这琴声像奔腾不息的江河从我心中流

过！"不管伯牙心里想到什么，钟子期都能准确地说出他的心意。钟子期去世后，伯牙认为世界上再也找不到知音了，于是，他把自己最心爱的琴摔碎，终生不再弹琴。

## 4. 重点词汇

民间乐器　笛子　琵琶　鼓　知音

## 5. 实践活动

### 说一说

（1）你的国家有哪些民间乐器？你会弹奏吗？

（2）中国的民间乐器与你的国家的民间乐器有什么相同点和不同点？

### Story of the Classical Chinese Folk Music
### ——*High Mountains and Flowing Water*

Boya was good at playing the zither, and Zhong Ziqi had a ear for music. When Boya played the zither, imagining the mountains in his mind, Zhong said, "Amazing! It's just like the towering Mount Tai standing in front of me!" When Boya was playing the music about water, Zhong said, "It sounds like the endless stream of rivers flowing through my heart!" Zhong Ziqi never failed to understand what Boya intended to express in his music. After Zhong Ziqi died, Boya believed that he could never find a bosom friend who could understand his music as well as Zhong. He broke his favorite zither and never played any instrument for the rest of his life.

## 4. Keywords

folk instrument   flute   pipa   drum   bosom friend

## 5. Activities

### Speaking

(1) Are there any folk instruments in your country? Can you play?

(2) What are the similarities and differences between Chinese folk instruments with those of your country?

**想一想**

（1）现代哪些乐器是中国本土的？哪些是从外国引入的？

（2）中国的乐器可以奏出和西方乐器一样的声音吗？

**听一听**

听中国民乐《十面埋伏》、《赛马》、《高山流水》、《梅花三弄》和《金蛇狂舞》，分辨这些民乐曲目各自采用了哪些中国乐器。

## 6. 自我评估

| | 😊 | 😐 | ☹️ |
|---|---|---|---|
| （1）我知道中国民乐历史悠久。 | | | |
| （2）我能说出至少3种中国民间乐器的名称。 | | | |
| （3）我能分辨至少2种中国民间乐器的声音。 | | | |

## Thinking

(1) What musical instruments are local Chinese ones? What musical instruments are introduced from foreign countries?

(2) Can the traditional Chinese musical instruments play the same sound as Western musical instruments?

## Listening

Listen to the Chinese folk music such as *Ambush from Ten Sides*, *Horse Racing*, *High Mountains and Flowing Water*, *Three Variations of the Plum Blossom*, and *Wild Dance of the Golden Snake*. Tell the musical instruments that have been used.

## 6. Self-assessment

| | ☺ | 😐 | ☹ |
|---|---|---|---|
| (1) I know that Chinese folk music has a long history. | | | |
| (2) I can say at least three names of Chinese folk instruments. | | | |
| (3) I can tell the sound of at least two kinds of Chinese folk instruments. | | | |

# 第八课　中国画

## 1. 学习目标

（1）了解中国画的典型类别，如山水画、花鸟画等。

（2）了解中国画的特点。

（3）了解中国绘画艺术与他国绘画艺术的异同。

## 2. 热身活动

**说一说**

（1）你喜欢画画吗？

（2）你的国家的绘画有哪些特点？

（3）你见过中国画吗？中国画有哪些特点？

## 3. 阅读课文

### 中国画的类别

中国画，俗称"国画"，主要表现形式为水墨画，是用毛笔、软笔或手指，用国画颜色和墨在帛或纸上作画的一种中国传统艺术，是琴棋书画四艺之一。

中国画可以分为人物、花鸟、山水三大类。

# Lesson Eight　Chinese Painting

## 1.　Learning objectives

(1) Know the categories of Chinese painting such as landscape or bird-and-flower painting.

(2) Learn about the characteristics of Chinese painting.

(3) Know the similarities and differences between Chinese painting and those of other countries.

## 2.　Warm-up

### Speaking

(1) Do you like painting?

(2) What are paintings like in your country?

(3) Have you ever seen any Chinese paintings? What are their characteristics?

## 3.　Reading texts

### Categories of Chinese Painting

Chinese traditional painting, known as "Chinese painting", whose main form is ink, is a traditional Chinese art using a brush, soft pen, or finger to paint on silk or paper with special Chinese painting color or ink. It is one of the four traditional artistic techniques, namely, music, chess, calligraphy, and painting.

Chinese painting can be divided into three categories: figure painting, bird-and-

　　人物画，画的是人类社会，表现的是人与人的关系。因为人有表情、性格，所以人物画是很深奥的绘画艺术。

　　山水画，画的是名山大川、自然风景，表现的是人与自然的关系。山水画不太追求外形相似，更注重意境和神韵。

　　花鸟画，画的是大自然中的其他生命，包括花、鸟、鱼、虫、禽兽等。

## 画龙点睛

　　南北朝时期有位很出名的大画家叫张僧繇，他的绘画技术很高超。

　　传说有一年，张僧繇在寺庙的墙壁上画了四条金龙，画得栩栩如生，简直就像真龙一样。很多人前去观看，都称赞他画得好。可是，当人们走近看，就发现四条龙全都没有眼睛。大家纷纷请求他把龙的眼睛点上。但是张僧繇说："如果给龙点上眼珠，这些

**76**

flower painting, and landscape painting.

Figure paintings depict human society and relationships among people. As human beings have expressions and personalities, figure paintings are very esoteric.

Landscape paintings depict rivers and mountains, natural sceneries, and the relationship between man and nature. Landscape paintings do not pursue to be alike with the objects in appearance, but artistic charm is always in the first place.

Bird-and-flower paintings are about other living things in nature, including birds, flowers, fish, insects, wild animals, and so on.

### Adding Eyes to a Dragon

During the Southern and Northern dynasties, there was a famous painter named Zhang Sengyao, whose paintings were of high quality.

Legend has it that one day, Zhang Sengyao painted four golden dragons on the wall of the temple. They were so lifelike that many people went to see them and praised him for his remarkable workmanship. However, when people approached, they discovered that there were no eyes on any of the four dragons. People asked him to paint eyes for the dragons, but

龙就会飞走的。"

大家听后都不相信，张僧繇没有办法，只好给龙"点睛"。他提起画笔，轻轻地给两条龙点上眼睛。过了一会儿，天空乌云密布，电闪雷鸣，被"点睛"的两条龙张牙舞爪地飞向天空。

人们被吓得目瞪口呆，一句话都说不出来了。

## 中国画的工具

笔、墨、纸、砚是中国书画不可缺少的工具，被称为"文房四宝"。它们不仅是书画的工具，也具有深厚的文化内涵。

毛笔是中国创造的，随后其影响力扩大到了朝鲜、日本等国家。毛笔的种类很多，根据绘画种类以及个人习惯的不同，用的笔也不一样。中国的书法和绘画，都与毛笔的使用分不开。

墨分为"油烟"和"松烟"两种。作为颜料使用起来会产生不同的效果，一种是植物做的，透明、细腻，但是时间长了会褪色；另一种是矿物做的，不透明，有覆盖力，很长时间都不会褪色。

中国画所用纸张的种类很广泛。其中宣纸产量高、品质好，其特性能把中国画的笔墨神韵最好地发挥出来。所以宣纸是最常用的国画用纸。

砚是磨墨用的。要求细腻滋润，容易发墨，并且墨汁细匀无渣。

## 4. 重点词汇

山水画　人物画　花鸟画　意境　神韵　栩栩如生　笔　墨　纸　砚

Zhang Sengyao said that if the eyes were painted for the dragons, they would fly away.

Nobody believed his words. So Mr. Zhang had to draw eyes on two of the dragons. He raised his brush and gently painted the eyes. After a while, the sky was cloudy, the lightning flashed and thunder rumbled, and the two fierce dragons flew away to the sky.

People were so frightened that they were at a loss what to say.

## Tools for Chinese Painting

Brush, ink, paper, and inkstone, known as the Four Treasures of the Study, are indispensable tools for Chinese calligraphy and painting. They also have profound cultural connotations. The brush was created in China, and then was brought into North Korea, Japan, and other countries. There are many kinds of brushes. The brushes vary for different types of paintings and personal habits. Chinese calligraphy and painting are inseparable from the use of the brush.

The two kinds of ink are "pine black" and "oil black". Each kind produces different effect. The former is made of plants, transparent and delicate, but it will fade in a certain period of time. The latter, opaque and very dark in color, is made of minerals and can last for a long time.

There is a large variety of paper for Chinese painting, among which Xuan paper is the best with a high output. Therefore, it has become the most popular kind of paper for Chinese painting.

Inkstone is used to make ink. It needs to be delicate with moisture, easy to make ink, and the ink produced in the inkstone is supposed to be fine without any slag.

## 4. Keywords

landscape painting   figure painting   bird-and-flower painting   artistic conception
charm   lifelike   brush   ink   paper   inkstone

## 5. 实践活动

### 想一想

中国的绘画艺术有什么特点?

### 说一说

(1)中国画有哪几类?画中国画要用哪些工具?

(2)画龙点睛这个故事告诉我们什么道理?

(3)中西绘画有什么不同?

### 画一画

画一幅中国画。

### 想一想,说一说

你的国家有哪些出名的绘画作品?简单介绍一下这些作品。

## 5. Activities

### Thinking

What characteristics does Chinese painting have?

### Speaking

(1) How many categories can Chinese painting be divided into? What are they? What are the tools for Chinese painting?

(2) What kind of lesson have you learned from the story "Adding Eyes to a Dragon"?

(3) What are the differences between Chinese painting and Western painting?

### Drawing

Paint a Chinese painting.

### Thinking and Speaking

Do you know any famous paintings of your country? Introduce them briefly.

## 6. 自我评估

| | 😊 | 😐 | ☹️ |
|---|---|---|---|
| （1）我了解中国画的常见类型。 | | | |
| （2）我知道中国画的基本特点。 | | | |
| （3）我会画中国画。 | | | |

## 6. Self-assessment

| | 🙂 | 😐 | 🙁 |
|---|---|---|---|
| (1) I can distinguish the usual categories of Chinese painting. | | | |
| (2) I know the basic characteristics of Chinese painting. | | | |
| (3) I can paint a Chinese painting. | | | |

# 第九课　中国航天事业

## 1. 学习目标

（1）了解中国航天事业。

（2）了解杨利伟和他的事迹。

（3）体验模拟航天。

## 2. 热身活动

**说一说**

（1）你喜欢航天吗?

（2）你想过当宇航员吗?

（3）你想去宇宙旅行吗?

## 3. 阅读课文

### 杨利伟——中国进入太空的第一人

杨利伟是中国进入太空的第一人。2003年10月15日北京时间9时，杨利伟乘坐由长征二号F火箭运载的神舟五号飞船首次进入太空。从此以后，中国成为第三个掌握载人航天技术的国家。

10月16日，杨利伟成了全国人民心目中的民族英雄。那天，他回到北京航天城时已经是晚上。两个小时太空旅行的极度疲劳还没有消除，他就给训练航天员的教员们一个个

# Lesson Nine　Chinese Aerospace Projects

## 1. Learning objectives

(1) Learn about China's aerospace projects.

(2) Know Yang Liwei and his deeds.

(3) Experience simulating aerospace.

## 2. Warm-up

### Speaking

(1) Are you interested in aeronautics?

(2) Have you ever thought of being an astronaut?

(3) Do you dream of traveling in space?

## 3. Reading texts

### China's First Man in Space——Yang Liwei

Yang Liwei is the first Chinese in space. At nine o'clock, Beijing time on the 15th of October, 2003, Yan Liwei was sent to space on the Shenzhou 5 space craft launched by a Long March 2 F Rocket. From then on, China became the third country to master the technology of manned astronautics.

Yang Liwei became a national hero on October 16. It was at night on that day when he returned to the Space City of Beijing. He was not relieved from the fatigue of the two-hour space trip and began to telephone astronaut coaches and inform

打电话，向教员们汇报自己在太空的情况。而此时电视里已经都是他的新闻和形象，他却好像什么都没有发生一样。

　　一位老教员感叹地说："难得啊，难得。能在巨大荣耀面前，保持如此平常心态，正是优秀航天员应该具备的素质。"

　　是的，面对巨大的荣誉，杨利伟没有居功自傲，也没有忘记航天员的神圣使命，他还是和平常一样，用平淡的态度对待一切。

　　他的亲人也成了新闻人物，甚至儿子小宁康也被众多媒体包围，但他要求媒体不要宣传，希望大家用平常心看待他和他的家人。

## 中国航天发展里程碑

　　1970年，东方红一号——中国第一颗人造地球卫星成功升空。

　　2003年10月15日，中国神舟五号载人飞船升空，中国成为第三个掌握载人航天技术的国家。

　　2007年10月24日18时05分，随着嫦娥一号成功奔月，嫦娥一期工程顺利完成。此后，神舟九号与天宫一号相继发射，并成功对接。

them about his trip. At that moment he was the center of the news, but he acted like nothing had happened.

One veteran coach exclaimed, "It's hard to come by. To be able to have a usual mind in the face of glory is the element of an excellent astronaut."

Indeed, in the face of glory, Yang Liwei took no pride and was committed to his sacred mission as an astronaut. He treated everything with his usual mind.

His family also became the focus of news; even his son Ningkang was surrounded by the mass media. However, Yang Liwei asked the media not to make a fuss and hoped that his family and himself would be treated with the usual mind.

## Landmarks for China's Astronautics

In 1970, Dong Fang Hong 1, the first Chinese artificial satellite was sent into orbit.

On October 15, 2003, China's Shenzhou 5 manned spacecraft was sent into space, making China the third country to master the technology of manned astronautics.

At 6:05 p.m., October 24, 2007, with Chang'e 1 heading to the moon, the Chang'e project completed its first phase. After that, Shenzhou 9 and Tiangong-1 were launched and connected in space.

## 中国载人航天事业的发展
### ——神舟系列飞船

神舟一号：1999年，实现天地往返的重大突破。

神舟二号：2001年，中国第一艘正样无人飞船。

神舟三号：2002年，载人航天安全性提高。

神舟四号：2002年，突破中国低温发射的历史记录。

神舟五号：2003年，中国首位航天员进入太空。

神舟六号：2005年，实现"多人多天"飞行任务。

神舟七号：2008年，航天员出舱在太空行走。

神舟八号：2011年，与天宫一号实现对接。

神舟九号：2012年，第一次入住"天宫"。

神舟十号：2013年，中国载人天地往返运输系统的首次应用性飞行。

## 4. 重点词汇

神舟　航天

## 5. 实践活动

### 想一想

（1）成为一名合格的宇航员需要什么条件？

（2）中国从第一颗人造卫星到载人航天中间经历了三十年，为什么隔了这么长时间？

（3）如果你是杨利伟，你最担心什么？

## China's Development of Manned Astronautics
### ——The Shenzhou Series of Space Craft

1999, Shenzhou 1: The entering into and returning from space.

2001, Shenzhou 2: China's unmanned space craft.

2002, Shenzhou 3: Improved safety in manned space technology.

2002, Shenzhou 4: Breakthrough in China's low temperature launching.

2003, Shenzhou 5: China's first astronaut in space.

2005, Shenzhou 6: More than one man and more than one day flying mission.

2008, Shenzhou 7: Astronauts walking out of the space capsule.

2011, Shenzhou 8: Connecting in space with Tiangong-1.

2012, Shenzhou 9: Astronauts inhabiting Tiangong-1.

2013, Shenzhou 10: First applied flying of China's manned space transportation system.

## 4. Keywords

Shenzhou space craft   aeronautics

## 5. Activities

### Thinking

(1) What are the qualifications to be an astronaut?

(2) It was thirty years from the launching of China's first artificial satellite to the launching of manned space craft. Why did it take such a long time?

(3) What would you worry about most if you were Yang Liwei?

（1）杨利伟有什么特点？

（2）你认为中国的航天事业还应该有哪些发展？

（3）介绍一位有名的宇航员，或者一个航天项目。

## 6. 自我评估

| | 😊 | 😐 | 😞 |
|---|---|---|---|
| （1）我能说出中国第一位进入太空的航天员的名字。 | | | |
| （2）我能说出第三个掌握载人航天技术的国家的名字。 | | | |
| （3）我知道有关中国航天的一些知识。 | | | |

**Speaking**

(1) What characteristics does Yang Liwei possess?

(2) What do you think should be done for China's astronautics in the future?

(3) Introduce a famous astronaut or a project of astronautics.

## 6. Self-assessment

| | 🙂 | 😐 | 🙁 |
|---|---|---|---|
| (1) I can tell the name of the first Chinese astronaut in space. | | | |
| (2) I can tell the name of the third country which masters the technology of manned astronautics. | | | |
| (3) I know some knowledge about China's astronautics. | | | |

## 1. 学习目标

（1）了解拔河的历史。

（2）了解拔河比赛的规则。

（3）参加一次拔河比赛，在比赛中体会团队精神。

## 2. 热身活动

**说一说**

（1）你知道哪些体育运动？

（2）你的国家有拔河这项体育运动吗？

（3）你知道怎样拔河吗？

（4）你有没有观看或参与过拔河比赛？

（5）拔河比赛让你印象最深刻的是什么？

## 3. 阅读课文

### 拔河比赛的规则

拔河是一项中国传统的体育运动。拔河比赛一般有两支队伍、一根绳子，绳子上系着红丝带。比赛一开始，站在绳子两头的两支队伍就需要尽最大努力把绳子拉向自己这方。时间一到，红丝带靠近哪一方，该方即获胜。拔河比的是力量，但只靠自己的力量是没有

# Lesson Ten  Tug of War

## 1.  Learning objectives

(1) Learn about the history of tug of war.

(2) Learn the rules of tug of war.

(3) Participate in a match of tug of war and experience team spirit.

## 2.  Warm-up

### Speaking

(1) What kinds of sports do you know?

(2) Do you have tug of war in your country?

(3) Do you know how to play tug of war?

(4) Have you ever watched or participated in tug of war?

(5) What impressed you the most about tug of war?

## 3.  Reading texts

### The Rules of Tug of War

Tug of war is a traditional Chinese sport. The tug of war competition usually consists of two teams, a rope, and a red ribbon on the rope. At the beginning of the game, the two teams standing at both ends of the rope will do their best to pull the rope towards themselves. When time is up, the team closer to the red ribbon wins. Tug of war is a competition of strength for the whole team and it is impossible to win

办法获胜的，要靠团队的力量。

## 拔河比赛的起源

你知道吗？拔河原来是一种军事练习。

在中国的春秋时期，楚国和越国经常发生水战，而楚国的水军总是输给越国。后来，一个叫鲁班的人，就给楚国设计了一种在战船上进行水战的兵器，叫作"钩强"。在进攻时，楚国的水军可以用"钩强"把越国水军拉到自己的船前，等到撤退时，再用"钩强"抵住对方的船，让越国水军没有办法靠近。后来，楚国常常在战争中获胜，很多国家纷纷模仿，训练水军使用"钩强"。

## 拔河得名的原因

针对水战的"钩强"训练，后来流传到民间，渐渐成了一种角力的游戏。人们把"钩强"上的钩子去掉，只剩下又长又粗的麻绳，然后在绳子正中插上一根大旗，在旗的两边划两条竖线，称为"河界线"。比赛时，以河界线为胜负标志，这就是"拔河"得名的原因。从唐代起，拔河就成为一项全民运动，一场比赛往往有上百个人参加。

by relying solely on your own strength.

## The Origin of Tug of War

Do you know that tug of war was originally a military exercise?

During the Spring and Autumn period in China, there were frequent water battles between Chu state and Yue state, and the navy of Chu state always lost. Later, a man named Luban designed a kind of weapon for water battle used on the battleship of Chu state. It was called *gouqiang*. The navy of Chu state used *gouqiang* to pull the Yue ships toward their ships in attack. When the troops waited to retreat, they used hooks to hold each other's ships and made the Yue state's naval forces unable to get close. Later, Chu state often won the war. Many countries imitated them and trained the navy to use *gouqiang*.

## Reasons for the Name "Tug of War"

The *gouqiang* training for the water battles was later widespread and gradually became a game to compete with strength. People removed the hooks on the *gouqiang*, leaving only long and thick rope, and then placed a large banner in the middle of the rope. Two vertical lines on both sides of the flag were drawn as the river boundary. When the game was played, the river boundary was the symbol of victory and defeat. This is the reason why tug of war got its name. Since the Tang dynasty, tug of war has become a national sport, and there are often dozens of people participating in the game nowadays.

## 4. 重点词汇

拔河　团结

## 5. 实践活动

**想一想**

（1）怎样拔河容易赢？是穿摩擦力大的鞋子？还是让力气大的同学站在最后？为什么？

（2）拔河比赛的目的是什么？

**说一说**

（1）"钩强"训练和拔河比赛的区别是什么？

（2）你的国家有没有类似拔河的活动？规则是怎样的？

**写一写**

参加一次拔河比赛，将你看到的、听到的、想到的、感受到的写下来，完成一篇100字左右的作文。

## 6. 自我评估

| | 😊 | 😐 | 😞 |
|---|---|---|---|
| （1）我了解拔河比赛的规则。 | | | |
| （2）我了解拔河比赛的历史。 | | | |
| （3）我了解拔河比赛的目的。 | | | |

## 4. Keywords

tug of war    unity

## 5. Activities

### Thinking

(1) How can you win in a tug of war? Wearing shoes with more friction? Strongest classmates being placed at the end of the rope? Why?

(2) What is the purpose of tug of war?

### Speaking

(1) What are the differences between *gouqiang* training and tug of war?

(2) Do you have a sport like tug of war in your country? What are the rules?

### Writing

Participate in a tug of war, and write a composition of around 100 words about what you see, hear, think, and feel.

## 6. Self-assessment

| | 🙂 | 😐 | ☹️ |
|---|---|---|---|
| (1) I know the rules of tug of war. | | | |
| (2) I know the history of tug of war. | | | |
| (3) I know the purpose of tug of war. | | | |

## 1. 学习目标

（1）知道泥塑和面人的含义。

（2）了解泥塑和面人的制作方法。

（3）了解泥塑和面人的艺术特点。

（4）学会制作面人。

## 2. 热身活动

**猜一猜**

这些是什么？

**说一说**

（1）你见过泥塑或面人吗？在什么地方见过？

（2）泥塑有什么特点？颜色漂亮吗？样子可爱吗？

# Lesson Eleven　Clay Sculptures and Dough Figurines

## 1.　Learning objectives

(1) Learn about clay sculptures and dough figurines.

(2) Know how to make clay sculptures and dough figurines.

(3) Know the artistic characteristics of clay sculptures and dough figurines.

(4) Learn to make dough figurines.

## 2.　Warm-up

### Guessing

What are these?

### Speaking

(1) Have you ever seen any clay sculptures or dough figurines? Where did you see them?

(2) What are the characteristics of clay sculptures? Are they beautiful in color? Are they cute?

## 3. 阅读课文

### 中国传统手工艺——泥塑和面人

　　泥塑和面人是制作简单但艺术性很高的汉族民间工艺品。用粘土捏出造型的工艺品，叫作"泥塑"；用面制作的可以吃的人物、动物，叫作"面人"。每年春节，中国北方人喜欢在家里制作大量的面人，用来祭神或者拜访亲人和朋友。

### 泥塑的历史

　　几千年前，中国人都生活在一个个小的部落里，每个部落都有一个守护神。人们十分崇拜他们的神，于是用泥土捏出了神的样子，放在家中保护自己。

　　后来，人们十分喜欢用泥做成的各种物品，死后也想要带着它们，泥塑就慢慢发展成了丧葬品。

### 面人的制作

　　面人的主要原料是面粉、糯米粉，颜色来自于石蜡、蜂蜜等可食用成分。制作面人，先要制作面团。首先，将面粉、糯米粉混合，揉制；其次，添加颜色成分，经过防裂防霉的处理，制成柔软的各色面团；最后，用面团捏、搓、揉出人物或动物的身、手、头、衣服，再用小竹刀刻出脸部五官和衣服花纹。

## 3. Reading texts

### Traditional Chinese Handicrafts
### —Clay Sculptures and Dough Figurines

Clay sculptures and dough figurines, which are easy to make, are artistic folk handicrafts of the Han nationality. Crafts made of clay are named "clay sculptures", while those made of edible dough are called "dough figurines". People in northern China are keen on producing plenty of dough figurines at home during the Spring Festival, to worship their god or present them to their friends and relatives.

### The History of Clay Sculptures

Thousands of years ago, the Chinese lived in small tribes, with a patron saint in each tribe. Since people esteemed the saints very much, they made sculptures in the shape of saints with clay and put them at home to guard themselves. Later on, people loved those clay crafts so much that they even hoped to bury it with themselves after their death. Eventually, clay sculptures developed into funerary objects.

### Production of Dough Figurines

Major components of dough figurines are flour and glutinous rice flour. The colors are from such edible materials as paraffin and honey. The first step of making dough figurines is to make dough. Wheat flour and glutinous rice flour should be combined and mixed. Secondly, the mixture will be colored and treated with some anti-mold and anti-cracking processes, resulting in soft and colorful dough. Then, the processed dough will be modeled into bodies, hands, heads, and dresses of humans or animals. Finally, facial features and clothing patterns will be carved by bamboo knives.

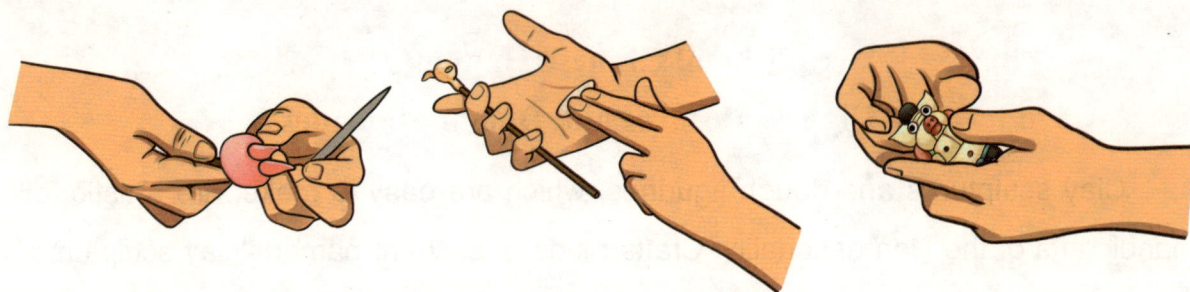

## 4. 重点词汇

面人　泥塑

## 5. 实践活动

**想一想**

面人最初的作用是什么？面人可以吃吗？

**说一说**

（1）泥塑最初是什么形状的？

（2）为什么人们死后也想带着泥塑？

（3）捏面人有哪些步骤？

（4）你的国家有类似泥塑或面人的文化吗？介绍一下。

**做一做**

学捏面人，向家人展示你的作品。

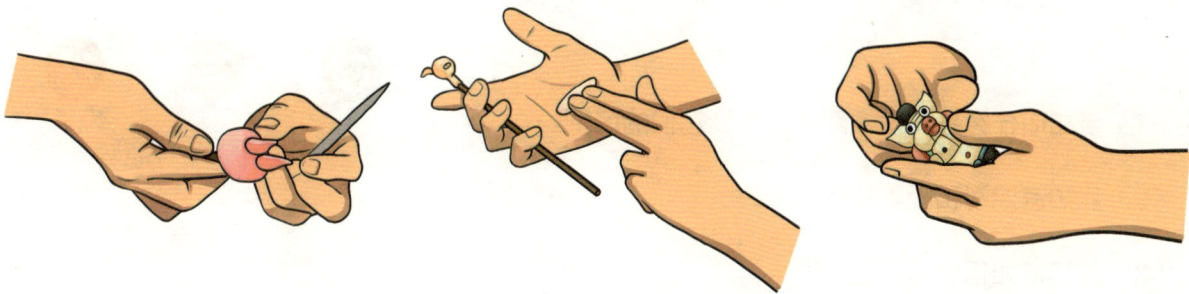

## 4. Keywords

clay sculpture    dough figurine

## 5. Activities

### Thinking

What was the usage of dough figurines originally? Can they be eaten by people?

### Speaking

(1) What were the shapes of clay sculptures originally?

(2) Why do people want to bring the clay sculptures with them after death?

(3) What are the steps of making dough figurines?

(4) Does your country have a culture of clay sculptures or dough figurines? Introduce it to your classmates.

### Practicing

Learn to make dough figurines and show your works to your family.

## 6. 自我评估

| | 😊 | 😐 | ☹️ |
|---|---|---|---|
| （1）我知道什么是泥塑、面人，以及它们的区别。 | | | |
| （2）我知道泥塑和面人的起源。 | | | |
| （3）我知道如何制作泥塑和面人。 | | | |

## 6. Self-assessment

| | 🙂 | 😐 | ☹️ |
|---|---|---|---|
| (1) I know what clay sculptures and dough figurines are and I can tell their differences. | | | |
| (2) I know the origin of clay sculptures and dough figurines. | | | |
| (3) I know how to make clay sculptures and dough figurines. | | | |

# 第十二课　茶

## 1. 学习目标

（1）了解茶在中国人生活中的重要性。

（2）知道中国人喝茶与外国人喝茶文化的相同点与不同点。

（3）品尝红茶和绿茶的滋味。

## 2. 热身活动

### 说一说

（1）你平时喝什么饮料？

（2）你的国家的人喜欢喝茶吗？什么时候喝茶？

（3）你家里人喝茶吗？

（4）你看见过中国人喝茶吗？你喝的茶和中国人一样吗？

## 3. 阅读课文

### 中国人的茶文化

中国有句俗语："开门七件事——柴米油盐酱醋茶。"对中国人来说，茶是一种不可缺少的日常饮品，也是中国文化的一个重要部分。茶最早起源于中国，之后又从中国传

# Lesson Twelve　Tea

## 1. Learning objectives

(1) Learn about the importance of tea in Chinese people's life.

(2) Know the similarities and differences of tea culture in China and other countries.

(3) Taste the flavors of black and green tea.

## 2. Warm-up

### Speaking

(1) What kind of drinks do you often have?

(2) Do people in your country like to drink tea? When will you drink tea?

(3) Do your family members drink tea?

(4) Have you ever seen Chinese people drinking tea? Is your tea the same as Chinese tea?

## 3. Reading texts

### Chinese Tea Culture

As an old saying in China goes, there are seven objects found after opening the front door: fire wood, rice, oil, salt, sauce, vinegar, and tea. For Chinese people, tea is an indispensable drink and also an important part of Chinese culture. Tea originated from China and then spread around the world. At the beginning of the 17th

到世界各地。17世纪初，茶通过英国东印度公司传到欧洲各国，很多欧洲人都养成了喝茶的习惯。

茶园

炒茶

## 喝　茶

茶树喜欢湿润的气候，主要生长在中国长江流域以南地区。

茶的种类有绿茶、白茶、乌龙茶（青茶）、红茶、黄茶和黑茶六类。

据说茶刚传到欧洲时，欧洲人不知道应该怎么喝茶。一个葡萄牙水手从中国带回了一些茶叶，他的妈妈把茶叶煮熟了，但是把茶水倒了，只吃茶叶。水手觉得很奇怪，问道："为什么只吃茶叶，不喝茶水？"妈妈回答："茶叶都这么不好吃，水还会好喝吗？我早就把那水倒掉了！"后来，水手说出了喝茶的方法，大家才慢慢接受了茶。

在中国的茶文化中，泡茶、品茶需要专门的工具和步骤。

常见的茶具：茶壶、茶杯和茶海（公道杯）。

century, tea was introduced to European countries through the British East India company and many Europeans adopted the habit of drinking tea.

tea plantation

frying tea

## Tea Drinking

Tea trees enjoy a humid climate, mainly in the south of China's Yangtze river basin. There are six types of tea: green tea, white tea, oolong tea, black tea, yellow tea, and dark tea.

It is said that Europeans did not know how to drink tea when tea was passed to Europe for the first time. A Portuguese sailor brought back some tea from China. Then his mother cooked the tea, but she poured the water and only ate the tea leaves. The sailor felt very strange and asked, "Why do you only eat tea leaves instead of tea?" His mother replied, "The tea leaves are so tasty. Will the water be good? I have fallen out of the water!" Then, the sailor taught people the way to drink tea, and tea was slowly accepted by Europeans.

In China's tea culture, tea brewing requires special tools and procedures.

The common tea sets include tea pots, cups, and fair mugs.

泡茶的步骤主要分为：温具（用热水冲洗茶壶和茶杯并沥干），置茶（把茶放入茶壶内），冲泡（按照1：50的茶水比例将水倒入茶壶，水温85℃左右），倒茶（冲泡好的茶先倒入茶海，再倒入客人的茶杯），奉茶（将茶杯递给客人），品茶（先闻香再品茶）。

茶中包含少量咖啡因，能够使人兴奋，所以喝茶以后会感觉舒服。一般不建议晚上喝茶，尤其是比较浓的茶。因为晚上喝茶会容易使人上厕所，却不容易睡着。

## 4. 重点词汇

茶　红茶　绿茶

The steps of making tea are mainly divided into: warm the tea set (rinse the teapot and teacup with hot water and drain it), put in tea (put the tea in the teapot), brew the tea (pour the water into the teapot according to the ratio of the tea at 1:50, and the water temperature is about 85 degrees Celsius), pour the tea (pour the tea into the fair mug first and then pour it into the guests' teacups), serve the tea (hand the teacups to the guests), and taste the tea (first smell the tea, then sip and taste tea).

Tea contains caffeine which can make people energized. So people feel comfortable after drinking tea. Generally speaking, it is not advisable to drink tea at night, especially strong tea, because it will make you unable to sleep and more likely to use the toilet.

## 4. Keywords

tea    black tea    green tea

## 5. 实践活动

**想一想**

（1）下图中分别是什么茶？

（2）为什么在置茶之前要温具？

**说一说**

（1）泡茶有哪些步骤？

（2）早晨、中午、下午、晚上可以喝茶吗？为什么？

（3）你的国家的人怎么喝茶？

**尝一尝，说一说**

泡一杯茶并品尝，回答下列问题：

（1）你品尝的茶是哪一种茶？红茶、白茶还是绿茶？

（2）茶是什么味道的？

（3）在什么情况下人们会喝茶？

## 5. Activities

### Thinking

(1) What kind of tea is it in the following pictures?

红茶

(2) Why should the tea set be warmed up before we make tea?

### Speaking

(1) What are the steps of making tea?

(2) Can you drink tea in the morning, at noon, in the afternoon or at night? Why?

(3) How do people in your country drink tea?

### Tasting and Speaking

Make a cup of tea. Taste it and answer the following questions:

(1) What kind of tea is it? Is it black tea, white tea or green tea?

(2) What is the flavor of the tea?

(3) In what situation do people drink tea?

## 6. 自我评估

|  | :) | :\| | :( |
|---|---|---|---|
| （1）我知道中国人喜欢喝茶。 |  |  |  |
| （2）我了解中国的茶文化。 |  |  |  |
| （3）我会泡茶。 |  |  |  |

## 6. Self-assessment

| | 🙂 | 😐 | ☹️ |
|---|---|---|---|
| (1) I know that Chinese people like drinking tea. | | | |
| (2) I know about Chinese tea culture. | | | |
| (3) I can make tea. | | | |

**图书在版编目（CIP）数据**

中国研习. 五年级＝China Study. Grade Five:
汉英对照 /吴勇毅主编；刘艳辉，王佳艺译. 一上海：
华东师范大学出版社, 2018
ISBN 978-7-5675-7908-8

Ⅰ.①中… Ⅱ.①吴… ②刘… ③王… Ⅲ.①中华文
化-小学-教材-汉、英 Ⅳ.①G624.201

中国版本图书馆CIP数据核字（2018）第144278号

# 中国研习（五年级）
## China Study (Grade Five)

主　　编　吴勇毅
副主编　刘　弘
策划编辑　王　焰
项目编辑　龚海燕　种道旸
审读编辑　顾晨溪
装帧设计　卢晓红

第三课"中国货币"的图片来源：除"交子"图片来源于百度百科之外，
其余图片来源于中国钱币博物馆（www.cnm.com.cn）。

出版发行　华东师范大学出版社
社　　址　上海市中山北路3663号　邮编 200062
网　　址　www.ecnupress.com.cn
电　　话　021-60821666　　　行政传真 021-62572105
客服电话　021-62865537　　　门市（邮购）电话 021-62869887
地　　址　上海市中山北路3663号华东师范大学校内先锋路口
网　　店　http://hdsdcbs.tmall.com/

印刷者　上海书刊印刷有限公司
开　　本　889×1194　16开
印　　张　7.25
字　　数　100千字
版　　次　2018年8月第1版
印　　次　2018年8月第1次
书　　号　ISBN 978-7-5675-7908-8/G·11238
定　　价　38.00元

出版人　王　焰

（如发现本版图书有印订质量问题,请寄回本社客服中心调换或电话021-62865537联系）